PM/AM

New and Selected

Poems

by LINDA PASTAN

PM/AM

New and Selected

Poems

LINDA PASTAN

W · W · NORTON & COMPANY · NEW YORK · LONDON

I would like to thank the following magazines in which these new poems first appeared: *The Atlantic Monthly*—Mosaic; *The American Poetry Review*—Dido's Farewell; *Field*—Ark; *The Georgia Review*—PM/AM, The Printer, We Come to Silence; *The Iowa Review*—In the Middle of a Life; *The Missouri Review*—Instructions to the Reader; *The New Republic*—Detail from the Altarpiece at Ghent; *Poet Lore*—Monet's Irises, The Moss Palace; *Poetry*—Crimes, I am Learning to Abandon the World, Lists, Waking, Waterfall; *Tri Quarterly*—After You Left, A Name, Salt.

The text of this book is composed in 10/13 Caledonia, with display type set in Bulmer.
Manufacturing by The Maple-Vail Book Manufacturing Group.

Library of Congress Cataloging in Publication Data

Pastan, Linda, 1932–
    PM/AM, new and selected poems.

    I. Title.   II. Title: PM/AM, new and
selected poems.   III. Post meridiem/Ante
meridiem, new and selected poems.
PS3566.A775P6   1982   811'.54   82–8015
                                           AACR2

ISBN 0-393-01638-2

ISBN 0-393-30055-2 (pbk.)

W. W. Norton & Company, Inc., 500 Fifth Avenue, New York, NY 10110
W. W. Norton & Company Ltd., 10 Coptic Street, London WC1A 1PU
    4 5 6 7 8 9 0

for Rachel

Contents

Aspects of Eve   37

The Five Stages of Grief   61

Waiting for My Life 83

PM/AM

New and Selected

Poems

Instructions to the Reader

Come. Suspend
willingly or not
your disbelief
and with empty pockets
enter the room
of the story.
Warm your fingers
at this candle
which is only the stub
of a dream
and at any time
may flicker
or go out.
Here fire consumes
itself
with paper
and pencil for kindling;
here a unicorn waits
in the corner
its musical horn
ready.
When I tell you
this story
is pure fact
you will want to leave
the room.
Stay awhile.
Evil is simply
a grammatical error:
a failure to leap
the precipice
between "he"
and "I."

There is also a beggar here
with a bowl of rice.
Fill your pockets,
hurry,
of the thousands of nights
there are only
a handful left.
At the end
the typesetter
will distribute
the type.
The letters will be divided
from all meaning,
separate as stars
whose small teeth chatter
but make no sense.
Only thus
is sleep possible.

New Poems

PM

The child is unreconciled
to the dark. Adrift
on her small bed
she listens
for voices down the hall
as if they were familiar waves
lapping at the unknown shore.
But her mother is almost silent.
The needle has dropped
from her hand,
and the only embroidery left
is the sky
stretched between window frames.
Her father loosens his tie.
He has used up
his small store of words,
and even his sleep will be burdened
by the heavy breathing of others.
This is how she remembers it:
the house creaking
as if it were loose
on its moorings;
the unnavigable dark.

AM

The child gets up
on the wrong side of the bed.
There are splinters
of cold light on the floor,
and when she frowns
the frown freezes on her face
as her mother has warned her it would.
When she puts her elbows roughly
on the table her father says:
you got up on the wrong side of the bed;
and there is suddenly
a cold river
of spilled milk.
These gestures are merely formal,
small stitches in the tapestry
of a childhood she will remember
as nearly happy. Outside
the snow begins again,
ordinary weather
blurring the landscape
between that time and this,
as she swings her cold legs
over the side of the bed.

Waking

In the first light,
in the first slippery light
we are born again,
and with the same struggle
every time. Thrown
from the hammock of sleep
onto hard ground
we lie there half amphibious,
watching our dreams move
helplessly away like fading
lantern fish.
There is nothing to do
but tie ourselves
into our shoes,
for they remember the way
from bed to table,
from table to door.
Our hands slip
into our pockets
where it is still dark,
still warm.
When they emerge
we cover them with gloves,
for blood runs sluggishly
through the terminal
of tracks at our wrists,
on its way to the far flung counties
of the heart.

A Name

FOR SUSAN WHO BECAME SHOSHANA

David means beloved.
Peter is a rock. They named me
Linda which means beautiful
in Spanish—a language
I never learned.
Even naked
we wear our names.
In the end we leave them behind
carved into desktops
and gravestones, inscribed
on the flyleaf of Bibles
where on another page
God names the generations
of Shem, Ham, and Japheth.

Homer cast a spell with names
giving us the list
of warriors and their ships
I read my children to sleep by.
There are as many names underfoot
as leaves in October;
they burn as briefly on the tongue,
and their smoke could darken
the morning sky to dusk.
Remember the boy of seven
who wandered the Holocaust alone
and lost not his life
but his name? Or the prince whose name
was stolen with his kingdom?

When I took my husband's name
and fastened it to mine

I was as changed
as a child
when the priest sprinkles it
with water and the name
that saves it a place in heaven.
My grandfather gave me a name
in Hebrew I never heard,
but it died with him.
If I had taken that name
who would I be,
and if he calls me now
how will I know to answer?

The Printer FOR R. H.

Baskerville, Perpetua, Garamond:
I thought you were naming a dance,
but the only minuet is typeface moving
across the page, and you in your apron bowing—
journeyman to the letter, apprentice to the word.
The smell of ink, like the smell of bread
signifies morning, a bleeding of color
at the horizon, the horizon itself
a line of boldface too distant to read.

In this world there are as many letters
as leaves, as birds, as flecks of ash;
whole armies of alphabets march across
margins of pavement, margins of snow.
Now there's a smudge on your forehead
where your hand strayed
making those architectural gestures,
the Pleasure of our Company is requested,
the ceremonial announcement of birth or death.

Your press is as fruitful as a wine press,
the sound of its motion like surf, hour after hour
reams of paper spreading their deckle-edged foam.

At night you distribute the type as carefully
as if you were placing your daughters in their beds.
Dark enters, a time before language,
but the sky is printed in white indelible stars,
with God's own signature—that thumbprint of moon,
like the printer's colophon
on heaviest Mohawk Superfine.

Detail From the Altarpiece at Ghent

The angels
in the corner
crowd this postcard,
ready to fly
wherever the mails
might take them.

They have the scrubbed faces
and the gauzy hair
of my daughter's friends
in high school chorus,
their cupped mouths brimming
with hallelujahs.

Wrapped in the reds
and golds of cherubim
those rough girls too
dreamed about boys,
and when Van Eyck was done
grew up and married them

and died. Today I pin
their picture to my wall
where the bronze notes
of the sun's great harp
can strike them
back to song.

Mosaic

1. The Sacrifice

On this tile
the knife
like a sickle-moon hangs
in the painted air
as if it had learned a dance
of its own,
the way the boy has
among the vivid
breakable flowers,
the way Abraham has
among the boulders,
his two feet heavy
as stones.

2. Near Sinai

God's hand here
is the size of a tiny cloud,
and the wordless tablets
he holds out
curve like the temple doors.
Moses, reaching up
must see on their empty surface
laws chiseled in his mind
by the persistent wind
of the desert, by wind
in the bulrushes.

3. The Flight Into Egypt

We know
by the halos
that circle these heads
like rings around planets

that the small donkey
has carried his burden
away from the thunder
of the Old Testament
into the lightning
of the New.

4. At the Armenian Tile Shop

Under the bright glazes
Esau watches Jacob,
Cain watches Abel.
With the same heavy eyes
the tilemaker's Arab assistant
watches me,
all of us wondering
why for every pair
there is just one
blessing.

Ark

The wooden coffer containing the tables of
the law kept in the Holiest Place of the
Tabernacle . . .

Oxford English Dictionary

FOR STEPHEN AND ELIZABETH

We all know
how the animals entered
that other ark
in twos,
even the promiscuous rooster
with his chosen hen,
even the snakes entwined,
remembering an earlier voyage
from Eden.
And Noah himself who knew
the worst of matrimony,
bitter words for breakfast,
complaints of sawdust
on the floor, nails underfoot;
at night her back turned,
hard and cold as the tablets.
Later the calls of mating
through the wet nights,
the tiny whir
of the hummingbirds' twin motors,
the monkeys' odd duet.
When the dove flew off
to find land
its mate perched on the railing,
the only creature
in that windy world alone.
I remember my wedding.
Standing before the ark

I thought of seas of matrimony,
of shipwreck.
When he stepped on the glass,
to recall the ruined temple, they say
I whispered: Man's dominion
over Woman. He smiled and shook his head
and later held a shard of glass
up to the light. In it
we saw condensed a perfect rainbow
and the white flash
of the dove's return.

Lists

I made a list of things I have
to remember and a list
of things I want to forget,
but I see they are the same list.
I made a list of items of need:
love and water on one side,
on the other the small flowers
that bloom without scent,
and it is like the grocery lists
my grandmother used to make:
milk and butter—dairy
on one side, meat on the other
as if they shouldn't mingle
even on the page.
My mother makes lists on tiny
scraps of paper, leaving them
on chairs or the seats of the bus
the way she drops a handkerchief
for someone to find, a clue
a kind of commerce between her
and the world.
And all the time the tree

is making its endless list
of leaves; the sky
is listing its valuables
in rain. My daughter
lists the books she means to read,
and their names are like the exotic
names of birds on my husband's
life list. Perhaps God
listed what to create
in a week: earth and oceans,
the armature of heaven
with a place to fasten
every star, and finally
Adam who rested a day
then made a list of his own:
starling, deer, and serpent.

In the Middle of a Life

Tonight I understand
for the first time
how a woman might choose
her own death
as easily
as if it were a dark plum
she picked
from a basket
of bright peaches.

It wouldn't be despair
that moved her
or hunger,
but a kind of stillness.
The evenings are full
of closure: the pale flowers
of the shamrock fold

their fragile wings, everything
promised has been given.

There is always
that moment
when the sun balanced
on the rim
of the world
falls
and is lost at sea,
and the sky seems huge
and beautiful without it.

I lie down on my bed
giving myself
to the white sheets
as the white sheets of a sloop
must give themselves
to the wind,
setting out on a journey—
the last perhaps,
or even the first.

Salt

This morning I spilled salt—
a delicate lace across the table,
and though I threw some
over my left shoulder,
the ritual gesture
of sowing seed, I knew
we would quarrel like this.
It was only chemistry
between us, and ended
you say. And I say
salt in the eye,

salt in the wounds,
a crystal of salt with facets
hard as a diamond's.
You ate your salt at my table
and like a tribe, confirmed
the contract between us.

The Devil detested salt,
but I'm with Homer
who called it Divine Substance.
They say The Heavenly Sophia
was the yellow of sodium,
the yellow of old women,
of burning salt,
and perhaps you find me old.
Once I tasted your sweat
upon my tongue (deer
at the salt lick)
and now my tears run
towards your mouth, leaving
a briny trail.
If you go now
I'll have my body
preserved for you in salt.

Crimes

Dear Disturber
of the Peace,
I accuse you of breaking
and entering my life—
a quiet room
whose windows you shattered
with light,
where there was space enough

for only one to sleep
and room for neither pain
nor promises.

For a brief time
I harbored you here,
both of us
fugitives of sorts,
though what I flee from
is harder to describe—
the way the sea looks when the wind
has lashed it black and blue,
the damage that happiness
can cause in its blind
tramplings. You left

the way you came
in a month of vagrant leaves,
the whole of winter shuffling
into sight, its white
hospital gown just visible
beyond the emptying trees.
Now a pot of yellow chrysanthemums
burns even at dusk
as if the sun were going down
at the horizon of my sill.
I choose again a life

of plants and vegetables:
the safety of peas in their pods;
the dark places in earth
where sweet potatoes lie
imitating stones; chrysanthemums.
Hear how the animals call
through the night,
each cry a riddle

whose answer you made simple:
there are poachers
everywhere.

Dido's Farewell

The rain is chronic
at my windows, and candles drown
in their own wax.
Abandoned by light,
even the filaments of stars
go black. This afternoon
I propped your drenched roses
up on sticks,
they look like young girls
on crutches now.

You left
a partial map
of your right hand
on every doorknob,
and I follow from room
to room, nomad
in my own house,
my own heart knocking
at my ribs, demanding
to be let out.

After You Left

Driving back to the empty house after you left
I could have been making my way back
to a past where I didn't know you,
or if we had met, we parted almost at once.

History would have to be changed only a little—
the fulcrum barely touched,
so that everything slides
to a slightly different position,
and the border of light hits the bare wall
instead of warming the plant
that is trying to blossom.

The house has the same wide windows,
the same dark floors, but now
it is merely a maze of rooms leading to
no place particular. And my days
will burn randomly, the way wax burns
in a dish without a wick, my days
will be like petals, losing
the stem that forms them into a flower
so there is only scent, only the vague
promise of sensuality, and even that
lasts only a moment.

I Am Learning to Abandon the World

I am learning to abandon the world
before it can abandon me.
Already I have given up the moon
and snow, closing my shades
against the claims of white.
And the world has taken
my father, my friends.
I have given up melodic lines of hills,
moving to a flat, tuneless landscape.
And every night I give my body up
limb by limb, working upwards
across bone, towards the heart.
But morning comes with small
reprieves of coffee and birdsong.

A tree outside the window
which was simply shadow moments ago
takes back its branches twig
by leafy twig.
And as I take my body back
the sun lays its warm muzzle on my lap
as if to make amends.

Monet's Irises

These flowers
have dreamed themselves
back into pure color—
the greens
of undivided water,
the formless
greens of meadow
just as God said:
Let there be
Irises.

The Moss Palace

At Kokodera you saw
as many kinds of moss
as there are names for snow
among the eskimos,
and the moss lay in deep banks
like snow. You tell me
of soft jade
between the stones,
of fur on the north side of trees,
of wild pincushions
at the edge of a stream, as smooth
as the pads of an animal's paw

when it rests its tamed head
upon your lap.

Moss serves no purpose
the gardener says, neglect your lawn
and moss will overtake it.
I want to be overtaken by moss,
to walk in my bare feet
on twenty different kinds,
to move from the hardness of rock
to sudden velvet and sink
the way I sink in the green of your eyes
when you speak of going with me
to Japan, when the place
where my body stops
and yours begins
is moss.

Water Wheel

1.

Afraid of sleep
the child asks
for one more drink of water.

2.

You hold my face between your two hands
as steadily as if I were a cup
about to spill.

3.

Remember this morning how the ocean's edge
unraveled at our feet, tangling us
in its accidental lace?

4.

You said we know what water is
although we never swim
in other oceans.

5.

Sometimes I dream of sitting in a waterfall,
of letting it churn like white fur
over my naked shoulders.

6.

It was fidelity you meant,
the stillness at the center
of the whirlpool.

7.

The waves are taking
our island inch by inch,
an army that will overrun us soon.

8.

You want a life
as simple as a cup
of rain,

9.

but see
how my reflection wavers
even in this glass.

10.

I think you'd throw cold water
in my face
to wash temptation out.

11.

The waterfalls
of sleep tumble
over us.

12.

I ask
for one more icy sip
of water.

We Come to Silence

We come to silence slowly.
Washed into the world
on a wave of sound
we leave it later with closed mouths,
our tongues grown heavy
as stones to anchor us
in earth. Now we hear
wind in the noisy leaves,
a hubbub of water
over the rocks,
the musical warfare
of the birds.
Consider the ear
shaped like the bass clef
but empty.
Consider the spaces between stars,
soliloquies of light.
It is almost time
to hush the children,
to quiet the dogs.
Even your words grow muffled
in my hair, soon
it will be only touch

I know you by.
These are the corridors
of silence; enter
on tiptoe.
Here Orpheus sleeps,
his harp unstrung.
Here the sound
a leaf makes
falling to ground
may deafen us.

A Perfect

Circle of Sun

Arcadia

There is always a bare house,
one cumulous tree balanced
at the rim of the second story,
emblematic fields the color of change.
We almost find it beyond
the drawn shade of the bus,
beyond the drawn eyelid where light flickers westward,
at the far end of the train whistle
as we travel with George Willard,
with Nick Carroway, travel
towards Christmas and a house
wrapped as safely in scenery
as the corn in its layers of husk.
Birds fly past the chimney,
grow smaller,
disappear as the house disappears around
the flung arm of the road—
solid as a dream at the moment of waking.

Writing While My Father Dies

There is not a poem in sight,
only my father running out
upstairs, and me without a nickel
for the meter. The children hide
before the television
shivering in its glacial light,
and shivering I rub these words
together, hoping for a spark.

After X-ray

The bones are all there waiting their hour,
patient as hangers, pushed to the back of a closet
on which this flesh is hung just for a while.
I feel them come to the surface slowly,
rise like their image in the developer's tank,
waiting to break through skin. And what can death
do with these bones? Planted like dry pods
in the earth they bloom later, washed clear of blood
to shine somewhere like strung beads of coral.

At the Gynecologist's

The body so carefully
contrived for pain,
wakens from the dream of health
again and again
to hands impersonal as wax
and instruments that pry
into the closed chapters of flesh.
See me here, my naked legs
caught in these metal stirrups,
galloping towards death
with flowers of ether in my hair.

Notes from the Delivery Room

Strapped down,
victim in an old comic book,
I have been here before,
this place where pain winces
off the walls
like too bright light.

Bear down a doctor says,
foreman to sweating laborer,
but this work, this forcing
of one life from another
is something that I signed for
at a moment when I would have signed anything.
Babies should grow in fields;
common as beets or turnips
they should be picked and held
root end up, soil spilling
from between their toes—
and how much easier it would be later,
returning them to earth.
Bear up . . . bear down . . . the audience
grows restive, and I'm a new magician
who can't produce the rabbit
from my swollen hat.
She's crowning, someone says,
but there is no one royal here,
just me, quite barefoot,
greeting my barefoot child.

Skylight

I sit in a perfect circle of sun
in a room without windows
where pale walls grow stenciled flowers
and see the tops of real trees,
see real leaves flickering in the light
as the tongues of garter snakes flicker
or flattening under an east wind
as if they grew in rushing water.
I think of a ruined church in Rome
where a boy in a blue shirt threw sticks
at a wall that had disappeared
who knows when,

or of something I only read of,
a man whose stomach was a window
doctors gazed through at organs
opening for food like tropic plants
beneath the floor of a glass bottomed boat.
And here in the center of this house
deep under shingles, under tar paper,
under plaster pale as unsunned flesh
I see through one round skylight the real world
held up to the sun by its heels and moving—
it is like candling eggs.

At the Jewish Museum

"The Lower East Side: Portal To American Life,
1887–1924"

We can endure the eyes
of these children lightly,
because they stare
from the faces of our fathers
who have grown old before us.
Their hungers have always been
our surfeit. We turn again
from the rank streets, from
marred expectancies and laundry
that hangs like a portent
over everything.
Here in a new museum
we walk past all the faces
the cameras have stolen from time.
We carry them like piecework
to finish at home,
knowing how our childrens' sins
still fall upon the old Jew
in a coal cellar, on Ludlow street,
in nineteen hundred.

Emily Dickinson

We think of her hidden in a white dress
among the folded linens and sachets
of well-kept cupboards, or just out of sight
sending jellies and notes with no address
to all the wondering Amherst neighbors.
Eccentric as New England weather
the stiff wind of her mind, stinging or gentle,
blew two half-imagined lovers off.
Yet legend won't explain the sheer sanity
of vision, the serious mischief
of language, the economy of pain.

Passover

1.

I set my table with metaphor:
the curling parsley—green sign nailed to the doors
of God's underground; salt of desert and eyes;
the roasted shank bone of a Pascal lamb,
relic of sacrifice and bleating spring.
Down the long table, past fresh shoots of a root
they have been hacking at for centuries,
you hold up the unleavened bread—a baked scroll
whose wavy lines are indecipherable.

2.

The wise son and the wicked, the simple son
and the son who doesn't ask, are all my son
leaning tonight as it is written,
slouching his father calls it. His hair is long:
hippie hair, hassid hair, how strangely alike
they seem tonight.
                    First Born, a live child cried

among the bulrushes, but the only root
you know stirs between your legs, ready
to spill its seed in gentile gardens.
And if the flowers be delicate and fair
I only mind this one night of the year
when far beyond the lights of Jersey
Jerusalem still beckons us, in tongues.

3.

What black-throated bird
in a warm country
sings spirituals,
sings spirituals
to Moses now?

4.

One exodus prefigures the next.
The glaciers fled before hot whips of air.
Waves bowed at God's gesture
for fugitive Israel to pass;
while fish, caught then behind windows
of water, remembered how their brothers once
pulled themselves painfully from the sea,
willing legs to grow
from slanted fins.
Now the blossoms pass from April's tree,
refugee raindrops mar the glass,
borders are transitory.
And the changling gene, still seeking
stone sanctuary, moves on.

5.

Far from Egypt, I have sighted blood,
have heard the throaty mating of frogs.
My city knows vermin, animals loose in hallways,

boils, sickness, hail.
In the suburban gardens
seventeen-year locusts rise
from their heavy beds
in small explosions of sod.
Darkness of newsprint.
My son, my son.

To a Second Son

Now you embrace chameleons
changing color yourself with the scenery,
white with me and my white questions,
muted under a sky bruised
black and blue.

You feed your lizards
moths, plundered each evening
from the porch light
while my shudder records
as accurately as a seismograph
the distance between us.

Peter, we have given you
these hand me downs:
your brother's half used sweater,
your father's reel,
and all my old faults
drowned once like a bagful of cats.

They have washed up twenty years downstream
bloated and mewing, to plague
the perfect body you will grow into,
shaking all of us delicately off.

There Is a Figure in Every Landscape

There is a figure in every landscape—
a boy at the other end of the pier,
a woman picking dandelions for salad
who leaves a kneeprint hidden in the grass
like the watermark on whitest paper.
That crooked branch is really a girl's arm
sunned to the very color of the bark,
an oval leaf conceals an oval eye:
children are climbing here, or have been.
Even in Adam's garden in the green
newness of unused shade, distrusting
privacy, God placed a sleeping woman.

Libation, 1966

We used to sacrifice young girls,
killing them like does
on rocky altars
they themselves had kept
tidy as kitchens.

Moloch took babies,
picked them early
from their mother's limbs
like green fruit,
spat out the pits.

It always was for some necessity,
fat harvest,
rain,
wind for a flaccid ocean, sails
flapping like gull's wings towards Troy.

Now we give young men.
They dance as delicately
as any bull boy,
with bayonette,
in a green maze,
under a sky as hot as Crete.

After Reading Nelly Sachs

Poetry has opened all my pores,
and pain as colorless as gas
moves in. I notice now the bones
that weld my child together
under her fragile skin; the crowds
of unassuming leaves that wait
on every corner for burning;
even your careless smile—bright teeth
that surely time will cut through
like a rough knife kerneling corn.

Between Generations

I left my father in a wicker basket
on other people's doorsteps.
Now I wait to be adopted by children,
wait in a house far between generations
with night rising faster
than the moon.

I dream of Regan laughing on her father's lap
behind the castle.
I laughed once in my father's face,
and he laughed and the two laughters
locked like bumpers
that still rust away between us.

My children fill the house with departures.
Zippers close, trunks close, wire hangers jump
on the empty pole—ghosts without their sheets.
And I ask what strict gravity
pushes love down the steep incline
from father to child, always down?

October Funeral

FOR AG

The world is shedding
its thousand skins.
The snake goes naked,
and the needles of the pine fall out
like the teeth of a comb I broke
upon your hair last week.
The ghosts of dead leaves
haunt no one. Impossible
to give you to the weather,
to leave you locked in a killed tree.
No metaphysic has prepared us
for the simple act of turning
and walking away.

Journey's End

How hard we try to reach death safely,
luggage intact, each child accounted for,
the wounds of passage quickly bandaged up.
We treat the years like stops along the way
of a long flight from the catastrophe
we move to, thinking: home free all at last.
Wave, wave your hanky towards journey's end;
avert your eyes from windows grimed with twilight
where landscapes rush by, terrible and lovely.

A Dangerous Time

November is a dangerous time for trees;
November is a dangerous time.
The leaves darken,
the sun goes on and off
beyond strange clouds,
a wolf is at the door.
Upstairs the children toss through dreams,
hearing the wind in the keyholes of sleep,
hearing the sirens circle the house like coyotes.
I have tucked them in with the wolf's own story,
how it grew from a cub, devoured the bride,
blew down the house of straw—
how this was natural.
Now my eldest walks the freezing hills
crying wolf, wolf.
He is a prophet, he has warned before
that the stars will rise like gooseflesh,
and a wolf is at the door.

Aspects of Eve

Rachel (rā'chal), a ewe

We named you
for the sake
of the syllables
and for the small boat
that followed the Pequod,
gathering lost children
of the sea.

We named you
for the dark-eyed girl
who waited at the well
while her lover
worked seven years
and again
seven.

We named you
for the small daughters
of the Holocaust
who followed their six-pointed stars
to death
and were all of them
known as
Rachel.

Night Sounds

When the clock,
like a moon, shows
the dark side of its face,
we reach
across cold expanses
of pillow

for speech.
In that silence,
a fox barks
from the next field,
or a train drags its long syllable
over a hill,
or the baby,
washed up again from sleep,
sends its vowels
calling
for their lost
consonants.

A Real Story

Sucking on hard candy
to sweeten the taste
of old age,
grandpa told us stories
about chickens,
city chickens sold
for sabbath soup
but rescued at the end
by some chicken-loving
providence.

Now at ninety-five,
sucked down
to nothing himself,
he says he feels
a coldness;
perhaps the coldness David felt
even with Abishag
in his bed
to warm
his chicken-thin bones.

But when we say
you'll soon get well,
grandpa pulls the sheet
over his face,
raising it between us
the way he used to raise
to Yiddish paper
when we said
enough chickens
tell us a real story.

Go Gentle

You have grown wings of pain
and flap around the bed like a wounded gull
calling for water, calling for tea, for grapes
whose skins you cannot penetrate.
Remember when you taught me
how to swim? Let go, you said,
the lake will hold you up.
I long to say, Father let go
and death will hold you up.
Outside the fall goes on without us.
How easily the leaves give in,
I hear them on the last breath of wind,
passing this disappearing place.

Wildflowers

You gave me dandelions.
They took our lawn
by squatters' rights—
round suns rising
in April, soft moons
blowing away in June.

You gave me lady slippers,
bloodroot, milkweed,
trillium whose secret number
the children you gave me
tell. In the hierarchy
of flowers, the wild
rise on their stems
for naming.
Call them weeds.
I pick them as I
picked you,
for their fierce,
unruly joy.

Folk Tale

1.

All knobs and knuckles, hammer knees and elbows
they were a multitude of two, man and woman
dwelling as one tight flesh. In hallways,
on stairs vaguely lit by twilight, in their own
meagre bed they would collide . . . veer off . . .
collide, like aging children aiming those
bumper cars, madly in Kansas Coney Islands.
Blue sparks jumped on their ceiling, lit her stockings
strangling his faucet, his fist plumbing
her shoulder's depth for blood. Until, as it is told,
they brought the cow into the house, straight from the barn,
oppressed for years with milk. They tied it,
lowing, to the icebox, pastured it
on rubber plants and dusty philodendrons.
They brought the horse in next, leaving the plow
like an abandoned aircraft, nose down
in rusting fields of corn. The pig, the donkey,
the rooster with its crowd of hens, they even

brought a neighbor's child complete with spelling words
and scales that wandered up and down the untuned
piano searching for roost as the chickens
searched and the cow, nuzzling the humming
frigidaire as if it were a calf.

2.

So they survived with all that cuckoo's brood,
hearing the horse stamp through the floor boards,
the donkey chew the welcome mat, and all night long
through tumbling barricades of sleep the yeasty
rise and fall of breath. By blue television light
they milked and gathered, boiled the placid eggs
that turned up everywhere, laughed with the child,
fed the pig, and glimpsed each other's rounded limbs
reflected for a moment in the copper
washtub or around the feathers of a settling hen.
And winter passed; and spring; and summer.
The child left first, all braided, for the school bus.
the cow died of old griefs. The horse dreaming
of harness, the pig of swill, the donkey
of what magnitude of straw, broke out one night
and emptied the ark. Man and woman leaning
on brooms stood at the kitchen door and waved,
saw through a blaze of autumn the cock's comb
like one last, bright leaf flutter and disappear.
Then jostling a bit, for ceremony's sake,
they turned and lost themselves in so much space.

Death's Blue-Eyed Girl

When did the garden with its banked flowers
start to smell like a funeral chapel,
and the mild breeze passing our foreheads
to feel like the back of a nurse's hand

testing for fever? We used to be
immortal in our ignorance, sending
our kites up for the lightning, swimming
in unknown waters at night and naked.
Death was a kind of safety net to catch us
if we fell too far. Remember Elaine
standing in April, a child on one hip
for ballast, her head distracted with poems?
The magician waved and bowed, showed us his
empty sleeves and she was gone.

Short Story

In the short story
that is my life
the mother and the father
who were there from the beginning
have started to disappear.
Now the lover repeats
his one line, and the plot
instead of thickening
as it might, thins
almost to blank paper.
There is no epiphany.
Even an animal whose cry
seemed symbolic
has lapped its milk
and gone quietly
to sleep. And though
there is room for a brief
descriptive passage (perhaps
a snowfall, some
stiffening of the weather)
already
it is dark
on the other side
of the page.

To Consider a House

"Eden is that old fashioned house we dwell
in every day . . ." Emily Dickinson

When Eden closed like a fist
around a penny,
like a flower whose petals contract
at the first touch
of weather,
when only fire was left to warn,
as fire warns the wild animal;
and even before Cain
had come to start
what we have never ended;
it was time then, for the first time,
to consider a house.
Before, they had rested
carelessly, naming a tree
then sleeping under it,
or sleeping first
and naming later. Now,
the soul shaken loose
from the body,
in temporary residence only
in their skin,
they dreamed the safety
of boxes within boxes,
of doors closing quietly
on doors.
They traveled East,
not following the sun
but drawn, as if by accident, back
to its source.
The animals too had fled, taking
only their names with them.
So as the birds learned,
they learned
to build of scraps,

of sticks and straws collected
along the way.
With the beaver they saw
what can be dammed up,
how to make use of all
that accumulates.
And like the bear they took
the hollowness of caves,
a shape to be confirmed
by the still untested womb.
In their own image they built their house:
eyelike windows, blank
with light; a skeleton of beams;
clay walls, crumbling a little,
as flesh was already learning
to crumble.
And from the hearth,
the smoldering center of the house, smoke
rose up the chimney
each morning, each dusk
making the leap toward God
that always ended
in cloud.
Only much later,
and hesitantly at first,
they thought to plant
another garden.

You Are Odysseus

You are Odysseus
returning home each evening
tentative, a little angry.
And I who thought to be
one of the Sirens (cast up
on strewn sheets
at dawn)

hide my song
under my tongue—
merely Penelope after all.
Meanwhile the old wars
go on, their dim music
can be heard even at night.
You leave each morning,
soon our son will follow.
Only my weaving is real.

Butter

You held the butter-
cup under my chin
and laughed: "get thee
to a buttery,"
chewing on a dandelion stem,
then tasting my
buttery fingers
one by one
and eying
my breasts as if
they too could
bobbing, churn
pure milk to
butter.
Yellow dress and
flowers, yellow
hair, the world
was melting butter
sweet and slick,
your hands all yellow
with the spilling
sun, desire
like the heated
knife through
butter.

Knots

In the retreating tide
of light,
among bulrushes
and eel grass
my small son teaches
my stuttering hands
the language of sailor's knots.

I tell him how
each Jewish bride
was given a knotted chaos
of yarn
and told to order it
into a perfect sphere,
to prove she'd be a patient wife.

Patient, impatient son,
I've unknotted shoestrings,
kitestrings, tangled hair.
But standing at high windows
enclosed in the domestic rustle
of birds and leaves
I've dreamed of knotting
bedsheets together
to flee by.

Swimming Last Summer

Swimming last summer in sun-kindled water,
hand in hand,
we had to surface dive to find
those cold currents
that run like harp chords counterpoint
to the lake's heat.

Still touching,
we swam between them, from cold
to cold, like children
in a field of scattered trees
running from shade to shade
for rest.

Now, in January,
the cold has risen to the top like cream,
curdling through the grassy shallows,
sharp as mica by the shore,
and at the lake's dead center
thick, opaque, reflecting neither casual cloud
nor shadows of a passing gull's wing.

Just so your eyes
rippling towards my shore all summer
now become glazed and cold,
your thoughts of me more sluggish than
some winter-dazed trout
swimming as close to bottom as it dares.

And maddened,
I long to beat your heat with my fists,
to chop through the freezing crust like an Eskimo
and fish you back
with nothing but string and a hook
and my remembered body
for bait.

Drift

Lying in bed this morning
you read to me of continental drift,
how Africa and South America
sleeping once side by side
slowly slid apart;
how California even now
pushes off like a swimmer
from the country's edge, along
the San Andreas Fault.
And I thought about you and me
who move in sleep each night
to the far reaches of the bed,
ranges of blanket between us.
It is a natural law this drift
and though we break it
as we break bread
over and over again, you remain
Africa with your deep shade,
your heat. And I, like California,
push off from your side
my two feet cold
against your back, dreaming
of Asia Minor.

Soundings

"And deeper than did ever plummet sound
I'll drown my book."

Shakespeare: *The Tempest*

If you drop a closed book
into a pail of water,
will it open like one of those
Chinese water flowers,

and bloom?
Will the characters
who were simply jogging along
leap
from its pages and swim
out of the pail?
All these years the books
have stood mute
on their shelves,
spine to spine,
Lilar up against Lilith,
Odysseus landlocked
at last
between the Iliad
and Orwell.
I have walked through this room
eating an apple, thinking
idly about suicide. Now
like some casual God I point my finger
at one book, open it—
it jerks to life crying, shouting,
making jokes at my expense,
talking, talking.
(It is the aviary at night:
the birds sleep perched
upon shelves, and I come,
throwing off covers
lighting lights, until
they open wings like moulting fans
and sing and fly
away.)
I pace this room of shelves
where books sit in their open graves
upright,
like the early Japanese dead,
reducing the world to words,
the words to letters,

the letters to intricate traps
that trip me until I fall,
dragging a bookcase with me.
And I drown
in the loosed wave of language.

Sacred To Apollo

Sometimes I am Daphne.
My sleeves rustle
in the wind,
and I feel the green root
of the bay, nourishing
or aching with the season.

And I have been Niobe,
all mother,
all tears,
but myself
somewhere hidden
in the essential stone.

You say I write
like a man
and expect me
to smile.

Or you hold me as though
I would break;
and indeed I come apart
in your hands
like pieces of a vast
and unsolved puzzle.

Perhaps it is Apollo
I still flee from,

despite his music
and his healing ways.

Now I paint my mouth
red for blood,
and in its twistings,
secret as any river,
I am Helen again
and dangerous.

Aspects of Eve

To have been one
of many ribs
and to be chosen.
To grow into something
quite different
knocking finally
as a bone knocks
on the closed gates of the garden—
which unexpectedly
open.

Hurricane Watch

I saw once,
through the eyepiece of a microscope,
a blizzard of cells.
And at times
the hairs on my arm lift,
as if in some incalculable wind,
or my throat echoes
the first hoarse forecast
of thunder.

Some live in the storm's eye only.
I rise and fall
with the barometer,
holding on for my life.
Here, in a storm cellar
of flesh,
pale as the roots I live on,
I read my palm
as though it were a weather map
and keep a hurricane watch
all year.

After Agatha Christie

in the locked room
what cannot happen
happens again
shaped to the size
of a keyhole
death comes reassuring
choosing someone
no one will miss
now everything becomes
a clue
the moon has left
footprints
all over the rug
the tree outside
the window
hides behind
its false beard
of leaves
who did what
precisely when
slyly the clock stops
the blood smells of ink

the revolver shows
its pearl handle
at the end the facts
click into place
comfortably as knitting
each answer marries
its proper question
even the skull
smiles to itself
as the detective tells
how the moon was pure
all along
the tree was merely
a tree
and only I
have no alibi
at all

An Evening Out

I have wandered into Chekhov
by pure accident,
mistaking the strokes
of my own heart
for the sound of an axe
against a tree
far away in the orchard.
But they have let me in.
The old family retainer
serves me, saying:
before the calamity
the same thing happened,
the owl screeched and the samovar
hummed all the time.
I hear no owl.
But drinking coffee, I dream

calamities of my own—
evenings like this, for instance,
my life which has gone by
as though I'd never lived.
I speak at random of the season
to a man in a grey vest
who mentions the weather.
But though he is polite,
it is clearly the dark-eyed girl
he admires most, and indeed
she is more slender than I.
Meanwhile, nothing much occurs.
We are waiting for something,
a shot, perhaps,
but here only a car misfires somewhere
in the empty street, and night
comes down over the sky
like the fourth act curtain
velvety and dark
finally falling.

At the Armed Borders of Sleep

touch me
says Harold
this is only a dream
so be quick
about it

It is a March day,
full of shadow.
Like an underground river a dream
surfaces
and is gone again
in shadow.

I move through cities
of sleep, past buildings
I lived in, or
thought to live in, and on
into the heart's suburb.
Here fear becomes simple.
Even the animals seem familiar,
they eat from my hand
while the roots of trees
tangle darkly with the roots
of my hair. But listen:
the wind is as violent as breath.
The hum of bees is the hum
of blood, swarming
out of a hive
of cells.

ah, be quick
about it.

There is light
assembling.
Perhaps it is morning
or the mother of morning.
I turn my back
on it.

At the armed borders of sleep
my dreams stand waving.
I brush my teeth,
eat breakfast,
dress.
The sun moves from darkness
to darkness, picking
its way
through the day's foliage.
I work at my desk,

drink tea.
They are still
waving.

Algebra

I used to solve equations easily.
If train A left Sioux Falls
at nine o'clock, traveling
at a fixed rate,
I knew when it would meet train B.
Now I wonder if the trains will crash;
or else I picture naked limbs
through Pullman windows, each
a small vignette of longing.

And I knew X, or thought I did,
shuttled it back and forth
like a poor goat
across the equals sign.
X was the unknown on a motorbike,
those autumn days when leaves flew past
the color of pencil shavings.
Obedient as a genie, it gave me answers
to what I thought were questions.

Unsolved equations later, and winter now,
I know X better than I did.
His is the scarecrow's bitter mouth
sewn shut in cross-stitch;
the footprint of a weasel on snow.
X is the unknown assailant.
X marks the spot
towards which we speed like trains,
at a fixed rate.

Eclipse

A few minutes past noon:
the birds begin their evening songs
and break for the trees;
the horse nods in its dimming stall.
Afraid of a truth that could blind
I turn my cold shoulder to the sun
and catch its shadow in a cardboard box
as though it were some rare bug
about to be effaced by the moon's
slow thumb. To catalog is not enough.
What did Adam know, naming the apple?
What do the astronomers suspect?
The sun like a swallowed sword
comes blazing back.
It is not chaos
I fear in this strange dusk
but the inexplicable order of things.

A Symposium: Apples

Eve: Remember a season
of apples, the orchard
full of them, my apron
full of them. One day
we wandered from tree
to tree, sharing a basket
feeling the weight of apples
increase between us.
And how your muscles ripened
with all that lifting.
I felt them round and hard
under my teeth; white
and sweet the flesh
of men and apples.

Gabriel: Nameless in Eden,
the apple itself
was innocent—an ordinary
lunchpail fruit.
Still it reddened
for the way it was used.
Afterward the apple
chose for itself
names untrusting
on the tongue: stayman,
gravenstein,
northern spy.

The Serpent: Ordinary, innocent
yes. But deep
in each center of whiteness
one dark star . . .

Adam: In the icebox
an apple
will keep
for weeks.
Then its skin
wrinkles up
like the skin of the old man
I have become,
from a single
bite.

The Five
Stages of Grief

Funerary Tower: Han Dynasty

"The meaning of the figures carrying babies
in their arms is not clear."

In this season of salt
leaves drop away
revealing the structure
of the trees.

Good bones,
as my father would say
drawing the hair from my face.
I'd pull impatiently away.

Today we visit my father's grave.
My mother housekeeps, with trowel
among the stones,
already at home here.

Impatient, even at forty
I hurry her home.
We carry our childhoods
in our arms.

After

After the month
in Sicily,
the ocean's edge unraveling
around our own
volcanic knees;
after the dark plums
that throbbed like fairy-tale hearts
in the woodsman's basket;
the voyage in another's arms

where we were innocent
as tourists
visiting familiar landscapes
for the first time

we come back
to our old lives
as to a heap of clothes
we have left in our closet,
and either they have shrunk
or we have grown fat
on the risen cream
of ease.
But soon our old possessions
cry out
like artifacts
not to be buried yet.
We are claimed

by our dishes, by their need
to be washed and dried
and put away;
by our mattress which like a pliant wife
has shaped itself
to our remembered bodies.
And at the edge of the grass
our deaths wait like domestic animals.
They have been there all along,
patient and loving.
We must hurry
or we may miss them
in the swelling dark.

Egg

In this kingdom
the sun never sets;
under the pale oval
of the sky
there seems no way in
or out,
and though there is a sea here
there is no tide.

For the egg itself
is a moon
glowing faintly
in the galaxy of the barn,
safe but for the spoon's
ominous thunder,
the first delicate crack
of lightning.

Voices

Joan heard voices,
and she burned for it.
Driving through the dark
I write poems.
Last night I drove through
a stop sign, pondering
line breaks.
When I explained
the policeman nodded,
then he gave me
a ticket.
Someone who knows told me
writers have fifteen years:

then comes repetition,
even madness.
Like Midas, I guess
everything we touch turns
to a poem—
when the spell is on.
But think of the poet after that
touching the trees
he's always touched,
but this time nothing happens.
Picture him rushing from trunk
to trunk, bruising
his hands on the rough bark.
Only five years left.
Sometimes I bury
my poems in the garden,
saving them
for the cold days ahead.
One way or another
you burn for it.

Adultery

"Between the motion/And the act/Falls
the shadow . . ."

T. S. Eliot

What does it mean,
this coming together at noon
when there are no shadows
to tug like the past at our heels
or to beat a dark path ahead of us
which we must follow?
True, my hair shadows your face.
But when we stand this way
at this hour

not even Euclid could take our measure—
we are a pillar of pure heat.
And if someone should mention to us
how Saint Peter healed
with his shadow
though we know pain
we would hardly listen.

In the Old Guerilla War

In the old guerilla war
between father and son
I am the no-man's-land.
When the moon shows
over my scorched breast
they fire across me.
If a bullet ricochets
and I bleed,
they say it is my time
of month.
Sometimes I iron
handkerchiefs
into flags of truce,
hide them in pockets;
or humming, I roll socks
instead of bandages.
Then we sit down together
breaking only bread.
The family tree
shades us, the snipers
waiting in its branches
sleep between green leaves.
I think of the elm
sending its roots
like spies underground
through any rough terrain

in search of water;
or its mirror image: Noah
sending out the dove
to find land.
Only survive long enough;
the triggers
will rust into rings
around both their fingers.
I will be a field
where all the flowers
on my housedress
bloom at once.

Soup

"A rich man's soup—and all from a few
stones."

Marcia Brown, *Stone Soup*

If your heart feels
like a stone
make stone soup of it.
Borrow the parsley
from a younger woman's garden.
Dig up a bunch of rigid carrots.
Your own icebox is full
of the homelier vegetables.
Now cry into the pot.
When he comes home
serve him a steaming bowlful.
Then watch him as he bites
into the stone.

Marks

My husband gives me an A
for last night's supper,
an incomplete for my ironing,
a B plus in bed.
My son says I am average,
an average mother, but if
I put my mind to it
I could improve.
My daughter believes
in Pass/Fail and tells me
I pass. Wait 'til they learn
I'm dropping out.

It Is Raining on the House of Ann Frank

It is raining on the house
of Ann Frank
and on the tourists
herded together under the shadow
of their umbrellas,
on the perfectly silent
tourists who would rather be
somewhere else
but who wait here on stairs
so steep they must rise
to some occasion
high in the empty loft,
in the quaint toilet,
in the skeleton
of a kitchen
or on the map—
each of its arrows
a barb of wire—

with all the dates, the expulsions,
the forbidding shapes
of continents.
And across Amsterdam it is raining
on the Van Gogh Museum
where we will hurry next
to see how someone else
could find the pure
center of light
within the dark circle
of his demons.

A Short History of Judaic Thought in the Twentieth Century

The rabbis wrote:
although it is forbidden
to touch a dying person,
nevertheless, if the house
catches fire
he must be removed
from the house.

Barbaric!
I say,
and whom may I touch then,
aren't we all
dying?

You smile
your old negotiator's smile
and ask:
but aren't all our houses
burning?

Ice Age

The Pterosaurus on the roof
spreads its ghostly wings
to shelter us.
In the thermometers
the mercury slides
to the bottom
making pools of silver—
we skate on them.
The world's weather is growing cold.
Already glaciers are moving
towards Maryland
where just now a light snow
started to fall,
and women are already knitting mufflers
which will not be thick enough
to warm our throats.
The snow is vague at the windows,
an early symptom.
Later the flakes will multiply,
the house will be wrapped
in a winding sheet of snow
snow like snuff in the nostrils,
like ash in the chimneys.
The children will build a house of snow
and disappear inside it.
Now wooly bears grow thick, black
mourning bands,
carrots burrow deep.
I have heard of miller moths
breaking into houses,
have seen my own breath ice mirrors—
they will need no other covering.
We must learn
the cold lessons

the dinosaurs learned:
to freeze magnified
in someone else's history;
to leave our bones behind.

Fresco

In Massaccio's *Expulsion
From the Garden*
how benign the angel seems,
like a good civil servant
he is merely enforcing
the rules. I remember
these faces from Fine Arts 13.
I was young enough then
to think that the loss of innocence
was just about Sex.
Now I see Eve covering
her breasts with her hands
and I know it is not to hide them
but only to keep them
from all she must know
is to follow from Abel
on one, Cain on the other.

March

It is a season
of divorce.
February ends
abruptly.
Oak trees which have fiercely
held to their leaves
all winter
suddenly

let go.
Our friends
tear apart.

We married so young.
I think of pictures
of Asian princes
betrothed at five,
their enormous eyes
accepting anything.

In the woods
dogs nose among emptied burrows,
bark at the silence.
Don't leave now.
We have almost
survived
our lives.

Bicentennial Winter

The only revolution is among the oaks
here in the woods;
their mutinous leaves
refuse to fall, despite
the laws of season
and of gravity.
Red-coated cardinals hide
among those leaves.
Red bird, cold weather
the farmers say.
Know us by our myths.
I think of the mutinous
Puritans who taught us
that all things break.
We have forgotten that,

disenchanted;
amazed as children told
for the first time
how they were conceived.
Still the mind moves
continually west, following
paths beaten by the sun,
risking ambush
and early darkness.
On Sundays, driving
past frontiers
lit by milkweed
let us find what wilderness
is left. Deep in the woods
it's possible to see the cruelties
between fox and rabbit
and their mutual beauty;
to study the creeks:
how the citizenry of small stones
is washed in waters that run
to the Potomac,
still clear in places,
in places muddy.
Today the river's a frozen slate,
a tabula rasa. It tempts us
as it did two hundred winters ago
to dare the dangerous
freedom
of the skater.

Final

I studied
so long
for my life
that this morning when I waken

to it as if for the first time
someone is already walking
down the aisle
collecting the papers.

And indeed
all of the relevant blanks
have been filled in
with children lost
and found and lost again,
with meals served
and eaten
and cleared away.

Only one page remains
empty, though it
is the hardest of all.
Its blanks are as wide
as hospital corridors,
each of its question marks
is the shape
of a noose.

For I have been accused
of cheating, of writing
the same line
over and over again,
and once when I brushed my hair
sparks flew out
igniting
more than I intended.

Now is the time
for the shuffling of chairs,
the scribbling of excuses
on the margins. I did my best
but there were handicaps:

a low pain threshold,
so many words I couldn't choose
between them.

I studied
so long
for my life,
and all the time
morning had been parked
outside my window,
one wheel of the sun
resting against the curb.

Can so much light
be simply
to read by?
I open the curtain
to see,
just as the test
is over.

Old Woman

In the evening
my griefs come to me
one by one.
They tell me what I had hoped to forget.
They perch on my shoulders
like mourning doves.
They are the color
of light fading.

In the day
they come back
wearing disguises.

I rock and rock
in the warm amnesia of sun.
When my griefs sing to me
from the bright throats of thrushes
I sing back.

Caroline

She wore
her coming death
as gracefully
as if it were a coat
she'd learned to sew.
When it grew cold enough
she'd simply button it
and go.

Consolations

Listen:
language does the best it can.
I speak

the dog whines
and in the changeling trees
late bees mumble, vague

as voices
barely heard
from the next room.

Later
the consolations
of silence.

The nights pass slowly.
I turn their heavy pages
one by one

licking my index finger
as my grandfather did
wanting to close the book on pain.

Afternoons smell of burning.
Already leaves have loosened
on the branch

small scrolls bearing
the old messages
each year.

You touch me—
another language. Our griefs
are almost one;

we swing them between us
like the child lent us awhile
who holds one hand of yours

and one of mine
hurrying us home
as streetlights

start to flower
down the dark stem
of evening.

Because

Because the night you asked me,
the small scar of the quarter moon
had healed—the moon was whole again;
because life seemed so short;
because life stretched before me
like the darkened halls of nightmare;
because I knew exactly what I wanted;
because I knew exactly nothing;
because I shed my childhood with my clothes—
they both had years of wear left in them;
because your eyes were darker than my father's;
because my father said I could do better;
because I wanted badly to say no;
because Stanley Kowalski shouted "Stella. . . ;"
because you were a door I could slam shut;
because endings are written before beginnings;
because I knew that after twenty years
you'd bring the plants inside for winter
and make a jungle we'd sleep in naked;
because I had free will;
because everything is ordained;
I said yes.

Arithmetic Lesson: Infinity

"In nature's infinite book of secrecy
a little I can read . . ."
William Shakespeare, *Antony and Cleopatra*

Picture a parade of numbers: 1
the sentry, out in front;
dependent, monogamous 2;
3 that odd man out, that 1 too many
always trying to break into line.
Numbers are subtracted, added

numbers fall by the way.
Some are broken into fractions—torn apart;
some assigned to stars, to crystals
of salt; to threads of water
on the ocean's dragging hem.
The proper numbers march together
their uniform buttons bright;
the rational numbers walk alone.
Every number on every clock repeats
its psalm over again
as minutes are numbered;
and children; and parcels of earth;
each sparrow as it falls;
each leaf after falling, before burning.
The negative numbers squabble
among themselves; imaginary numbers
count the number of kisses
that dance on the head of a pin.
And the parade goes on.
Each leaf of grass is numbered
just as it bends beneath
a numbered foot; each newt;
each spider's egg;
each grain of sleep caught
in each waking eye.
Pages are numbered as they turn;
dreams as they turn
into facts; the sun
as it rises on its fiery stalk
and as it sets.
But just as the end trembles into sight
the way the sea trembles
beyond the final dune
the steps of the marchers
grow smaller and smaller again—
the steps divide. Each number
hangs back, reluctant as a child

afraid of what he'll find
at the end of a darkened hall.
And though the destination
remains always at hand
the parade moves slowly on: 1
the sentry, out in front;
dependent, monogamous 2;
3

The Five Stages of Grief

The night I lost you
someone pointed me towards
the Five Stages of Grief.
Go that way, they said,
it's easy, like learning to climb
stairs after the amputation.
And so I climbed.
Denial was first.
I sat down at breakfast
carefully setting the table
for two. I passed you the toast—
you sat there. I passed
you the paper—you hid
behind it.
Anger seemed more familiar.
I burned the toast, snatched
the paper and read the headlines myself.
But they mentioned your departure,
and so I moved on to
Bargaining. What could I exchange
for you? The silence
after storms? My typing fingers?
Before I could decide, *Depression*
came puffing up, a poor relation
its suitcase tied together

with string. In the suitcase
were bandages for the eyes
and bottles of sleep. I slid
all the way down the stairs
feeling nothing.
And all the time Hope
flashed on and off
in defective neon.
Hope was a signpost pointing
straight in the air.
Hope was my uncle's middle name,
he died of it.
After a year I am still climbing,
though my feet slip
on your stone face.
The treeline
has long since disappeared;
green is a color
I have forgotten.
But now I see what I am climbing
towards: *Acceptance*
written in capital letters,
a special headline:
Acceptance,
its name is in lights.
I struggle on,
waving and shouting.
Below, my whole life spreads its surf,
all the landscapes I've ever known
or dreamed of. Below
a fish jumps: the pulse
in your neck.
Acceptance. I finally
reach it.
But something is wrong.
Grief is a circular staircase.
I have lost you.

Waiting for
My Life

Epilogue

Years later the girl died
no longer a girl,
and the old man fishing
in sullied waters
saw his one mistake
flash by—
but only for a moment.
The moon continued
its periodic rise and fall,
sometimes the shape
of a snow elk's horn,
sometimes a vague
repository of light.
Katerina married
someone else.
Robert, though only a minor character
grew into the hero
of another story.
And the house was rebuilt
by strangers.
Only the lake stayed the same,
its surface equivocal
as the pages of a book
on which everything remains
to be written.

Prologue

Nothing has happened yet.
The house settles
into its stones,
unoccupied;
the road curves
towards something—
away from something else.
A single elk bends
to the lake to drink,
or in the confusion of dusk
perhaps it is simply
an old tree
leaning over the water.
If there were voices,
their language would be
expectancy; but the silence
is nearly perfect.
Even the sun is motionless
before it takes that definite plunge
into the darkness
of the first chapter.

Dreams

Dreams are the only
afterlife we know;
the place where the children
we were
rock in the arms of the children
we have become.

They are as many as leaves
in their migrations,
as birds whose deaths we learn of
by the single feather
left behind: a clue,
a particle of sleep

caught in the eye.
They are as irretrievable as sand
when the sea creeps up
its long knife glittering
in its teeth
to claim its patrimony.

Sometimes my father
in knickers and cap
waits on that shore,
the dream of him
a wound
not even morning can heal.

The dog's legs pump
in his sleep;
your closed eyelids flicker
as the reel unwinds:
watcher and watched,
archer and bull's-eye.

Last night I dreamed a lover in my arms
and woke innocent.
The sky was starry to the very rind,
his smile still burning there
like the tail of a comet
that has just blazed by.

McGuffey's First Eclectic Reader

The sun is up
the sun is always up.
The silent "e"
keeps watch;
and 26 strong stones
can build a wall of syllables
for Nell and Ned
and Ann:

Rab was such a good dog,
Mother. We left him
under the big tree
by the brook
to take care of the dolls
and the basket.

But Rab has run away.
The basket's gone back to reeds
through which the night wind
blows; and mother was erased;
the dolls are painted harlots
in the Doll's Museum.

Where did it go, Rose?
I don't know;
away off, somewhere.

The fat hen
has left the nest.

I hand my daughter
this dusty book.
Framed in her window
the sky darkens to slate:
a lexicon of wandering stars.
Listen, child—the barking
in the distance
is Rab the dog star
trotting home
for dinner.

Friday's Child

We always called Cassandra
immature—the way she ran
through town with her electric hair
and torn clothes, telling us
what we already knew:
that regiments of clouds
were being formed
that could bombard us soon
with snow, could bury us;
that art is an equivocal gift;
that every flower awaited
its proper place
on our funeral wreaths.
We knew all that—
she was our own child.
But once betrothed to grief
what could we do but mourn?
We let her speak; and speak.
All words, anyway
are epitaphs.

Secrets

The secrets I keep
from myself
are the same secrets
the leaves keep
from the old trunk
of the tree
even as they turn
color.

They are the garbled
secrets
of the waterfall
about to be stunned
on rock;
the sound of the stream's
dry mouth
after weeks of drought.

Hush, says the nurse
to the new child howling
its one secret
into the world,
hush
as she buries
its mouth
in milk.

On the hearth the fire consumes
its own burning tongue,
I cannot read the ash.
By the gate
the trumpet flower sings
only silence
from its shapely
throat.

At night
I fall asleep
to the whippoorwill's
raucous lullabye,
old as the first garden:
never tell
never tell
never tell.

Letter to a Son at Exam Time

May again
and poems leaf out
from this old typewriter
shading the desk in half-light.
You at a college desk study different poems,
hold them warily by their dry stems—
so many leaves pressed to death
in a heavy book.

When you forget again
to call
it's poet and parent both
that you deny.
This is what I didn't know
I knew.

You woke up
on the wrong side
of my life.
For years I counted myself to sleep
on all the ways I might lose you:
death in its many-colored coat lounged
at the schoolhouse door, delivered
the milk; drove the carpool.

Now I catalogue leaves instead
on a weeping cherry.

It doesn't really weep,
nor do poets cry, so amazed
they are at the prosody
of pain.

You have a way with words yourself
you never asked for.
Though you disguise them
as best you can
in Gothic misspellings
there they stand in all their new muscle.
You will use them against me perhaps,
but you will use them.

The One-Way Mirror Back

1.

The pages of my books
rustled
with the same sound
my mother's skirts made
on her way
out the door.

And my father's mustache
bobbed
in the distance
like the old rowboat
across the lake—
only a bit absurd,
only a little dangerous.

2.

I didn't have a brother,
though long before me
there was a baby

they never speak of
for whom I named
my son.

And when it became clear
I would not catch the ball
or cut into the frog
they forgave me again
because I was just
a girl.

3.

I hoarded A's at school
the way I hoarded aces
when I beat my mother
at Gin. There was tea
for my sore throat and honey
and light the color
of tea and honey.

On the radio Stella Dallas
talked of her beautiful
daughter Lolly
in almost the voice
my mother used
to tell my father
how many games I'd won.

4.

the small glow
of the flowers we called
japanese lanterns

swinging
on their long stems
lit the summer dusk

later the countryside blew by
the back seat of the car
as we sang rounds

my father's voice
my mother's voice
mine

row your boat . . .
oh how lovely is the evening . . .
merrily, merrily

our three voices braiding
braiding
into one voice

5.

shut up
I playfully
told my father
once
and he did
for seven long
days

6.

One day I knew
the simplicities
of power, a lesson
the leaf learns
when it breaks
through its chrysalis
of bark, a lesson
the sap learns
rising
through all the laws

of gravity.
I learned this lesson
late.

7.

What I remember
hardly happened;
what they say happened
I hardly remember.
In the one-way mirror back
I see only that appetite
was harder to appease
than hunger, dreams
more persistent
than appetite, tripping
me down their drowsy stairs
until I rested
in my nest of bones
unhurt.

Waiting for My Life

I waited for my life to start
for years, standing at bus stops
looking into the curved distance
thinking each bus was the wrong bus;
or lost in books where I would travel
without luggage from one page
to another; where the only breeze
was the rustle of pages turning,
and lives rose and set
in the violent colors of suns.

Sometimes my life coughed and coughed:
a stalled car about to catch,
and I would hold someone in my arms,
though it was always someone else I wanted.

Or I would board any bus, jostled
by thighs and elbows that knew
where they were going; collecting scraps
of talk, setting them down like bird song
in my notebook, where someday I would go
prospecting for my life.

In Back Of

"I'm looking for things back of re-
marks that are said . . ."

William Stafford

In back of "I love you"
stands "goodbye."
In back of
"goodbye"
stands "it was lovely
there in the grass, drenched
in so much green
together."
Words that wait
are dark as shadows
in the back rooms
of mirrors:
when you raise
your right hand
in greeting,
they raise their left
in farewell.

Eyes Only

Dear lost sharer
of silences,
I would send a letter
the way the tree sends messages

in leaves,
or the sky in exclamations
of pure cloud.

Therefore I write
in this blue
ink, color
of secret veins
and arteries.
It is morning here.
Already the postman walks

the innocent streets,
dangerous as Aeolus
with his bag of winds,
or Hermes, the messenger,
god of sleep and dreams
who traces my image
upon this stamp.

In public buildings
letters are weighed
and sorted like meat;
in railway stations
huge sacks of mail
are hidden like robbers' booty
behind freight-car doors.

And in another city
the conjurer
will hold a fan of letters
before your outstretched hand—
"Pick any card . . ."
You must tear the envelope
as you would tear bread.

Only then dark rivers
of ink will thaw

and flow
under all the bridges
we have failed
to build
between us.

Meditation by the Stove

I have banked the fires
of my body
into a small but steady blaze,
here in the kitchen
where the dough has a life of its own,
breathing under its damp cloth
like a sleeping child;
where the real child plays under the table,
pretending the tablecloth is a tent,
practicing departures; where a dim
brown bird dazzled by light
has flown into the windowpane
and lies stunned on the pavement—
it was never simple, even for birds,
this business of nests.
The innocent eye sees nothing, Auden says,
repeating what the snake told Eve,
what Eve told Adam, tired of gardens,
wanting the fully lived life.
But passion happens like an accident.
I could let the dough spill over the rim
of the bowl, neglecting to punch it down,
neglecting the child who waits under the table,
the mild tears already smudging her eyes.
We grow in such haphazard ways.
Today I feel wiser than the bird.
I know the window shuts me in,
that when I open it

the garden smells will make me restless.
And I have banked the fires of my body
into a small domestic flame for others
to warm their hands on for a while.

Who Is It Accuses Us?

Who is it accuses us of safety,
as if the family were soldiers
instead of hostages,
as if the gardens were not mined
with explosive peonies,
as if the most common death
were not by household accident?
We have chosen the dangerous life.
Consider the pale necks of the children
under their colored head scarves,
the skin around the husbands' eyes, flayed
by guilt and promises.
You who risk no more than your own skins
I tell you household Gods
are jealous Gods.
They will cover your window sills
with the dust of sunsets;
they will poison your secret wells
with longing.

What We Want

What we want
is never simple.
We move among the things
we thought we wanted:
a face, a room, an open book

and these things bear our names—
now they want us.
But what we want appears
in dreams, wearing disguises.
We fall past,
holding out our arms
and in the morning
our arms ache.
We don't remember the dream,
but the dream remembers us.
It is there all day
as an animal is there
under the table,
as the stars are there
even in full sun.

The Japanese Way

Now I have been caught
in the karma of past lives . . .

Kenrei Mon-in Ukyo no Diabu,
                    12th Century

In this eastern light
I feel my eyes
slant shut. I kneel
on tatami at your feet
and with delicate
gestures of wood
take crab from claw
to feed you. How easy
to hide in the sleeves
of a kimona, to feel
the silk seduce
my very skin,
to let my strong sons

be my only measure:
mother and wife—
as when you hold me here
and I can see
in the raked sand
all the ocean I need.
But over the nightingale floor
made cunningly so the wood
sings at the joints
when enemies approach,
I hear instead my sisters
tiptoe near, freeing
their complicated wings
of hair.

The War Between Desire
and Dailiness

(Variation on a line by Robert Hass)

When you said "I think
I know your mind,"
you touched me
in the one private place
left. The heat
of those words ignites
my face, declares
a war between desire
and dailiness.
At the site of such longing
all order disappears.
I must summon arms:
spoons in the fists
of children, each beating
its own martial measure;
dates on the calendar marked

in blood for births, for deaths;
my only flag, a pillowcase
bleaching in the sun
on which no lover's head
has rested yet.
In the first moments of spring
I too am threatened
by thaw, deep underground.
Spring is the shortest season.
Let dailiness win.

Helen Bids Farewell
to Her Daughter Hermione

There is time
before I go
to mention the lily flowering
by the door—
how, when divided,
it multiplies.
I'm speaking now
of love.

There is time
to tell you
the only story I know:
a youth sets out,
a man or woman returns,
the rest is simply incident
or weather

and yet what storms
I could describe
swirling
in every thumbprint.

There is time
before I go
to show you the way
light slants
across a page
or through a doorway,
as if the darkness too
were vulnerable.

When the Moment Is Over

When the moment is over—
the light we have turned inward
the way as children we press a flashlight
into our own flesh
making each limb seem
to smolder—
when that light goes off
we are saved once more
by dailiness:
the sun has continued
its unbroken journey;
the sheets may need smoothing
as the forehead needs smoothing
after fever.

What we have learned
we continue to learn
as we continually memorize objects
deep in our pockets: the key
to a certain door; a coin
whose severe face
is worn to a smile.
And we listen for echoes
from the buried chambers
of the heart

whose messages are tapped out
in unbreakable code,
whose fires are stoked secretly
even as we sleep.

after minor surgery

this is the dress rehearsal
when the body
like a constant lover
flirts for the first time
with faithlessness

when the body
like a passenger on a long journey
hears the conductor call out
the name
of the first stop

when the body
in all its fear and cunning
makes promises to me
it knows
it cannot keep

November

It is an old drama
this disappearance of the leaves,
this seeming death
of the landscape.
In a later scene,
or earlier,
the trees like gnarled magicians
produce handkerchiefs

of leaves
out of empty branches.

And we watch.
We are like children
at this spectacle
of leaves,
as if one day we too
will open the wooden doors
of our coffins
and come out smiling
and bowing
all over again.

A Middle-Aged Poet
Leaves the Movies

You come out weeping
for Iphigenia, for all our scrape-kneed
vulnerable daughters, only half innocent.
You travel the used-up streets,
back to the house where one day
the winds of your life suddenly
went slack
as Agamemnon had his usual way.

Now you turn to "larger" issues,
brushing aside the small poems of the self
as if they were so many gnats.
The tea has steeped to darkness
in your cup; the sun steeps at the edges
of the sky: the stuff of poems, you think—
and wrestle instead with the Greek alphabet.
From Troy only the women's tasks are left:

tomorrow you'll wrestle bread,
kneading it with your large hands,
letting it rise slowly in some dark place
the way the poems must slowy rise
through all your darknesses.
You'll write how Iphigenia once played
among the small but perfect Aegean flowers;
she never grew middle aged.

Pain

More faithful
than lover or husband
it cleaves to you,
calling itself by your name
as if there had been a ceremony.

At night you turn and turn
searching for the one
bearable position,
but though you may finally sleep
it wakens ahead of you.

How heavy it is,
displacing with its volume
your very breath.
Before, you seemed to weigh nothing,
your arms might have been wings.

Now each finger adds its measure;
you are pulled down by the weight
of your own hair.
And if your life should disappear ahead of you
you would not run after it.

Weather Forecast

Somewhere it is about to snow,
if not in the northern suburbs,
then in the west,
if not there, then here.
And the wind
which is camouflaged now
by the perfect stillness of trees
will make some weathercock dizzy
with its fickle breath.
In the blood's failing heat
we wait for the verdict
of snow. You bite into an apple
with the sound boots make
crunching through
the first icy layers.
The whites of your eyes are cold.
The moons of your nails
are frozen mounds.
A single match striking
against the bottom of a shoe
is our only prayer.

blizzard

the snow
has forgotten
how to stop
it falls
stuttering
at the glass
a silk windsock
of snow
blowing

under the porch light
tangling trees
which bend
like old women
snarled
in their own
knitting
snow drifts
up to the step
over the doorsill
a pointillist's blur
the wedding
of form and motion
shaping itself
to the wish of
any object it touches
chairs become
laps of snow
the moon could be
breaking apart
and falling
over the eaves
over the roof
a white bear
shaking its paw
at the window
splitting the hive
of winter
snow stinging
the air
I pull a comforter
of snow
up to my chin
and tumble
to sleep
as the whole
alphabet

of silence
falls out of the
sky

There Are Poems

There are poems
that are never written,
that simply move across
the mind
like skywriting
on a still day:
slowly the first word
drifts west,
the last letters dissolve
on the tongue,
and what is left
is the pure blue
of insight, without cloud
or comfort.

Response

"a ban on the following subject matter: the
Holocaust, grandparents, Friday night candle
lighting . . . Jerusalem at dusk."

from the poetry editor of *Response*

It is not dusk
in Jerusalem
it is simply morning

and the grandparents have disappeared
into the Holocaust
taking their sabbath candles with them.

Light your poems, hurry.
Already the sun is leaning
towards the west

though the grandparents and candles
have long since burned down
to stubs.

Widow's Walk, Somewhere Inland

This landlocked house should grace a harbor:
its widow's walk of grey pickets
surveys an inland sea
of grass; wind
breaks like surf against
its rough shingles.

In summer the two grown sons
tie up here for awhile.
The daughter with her mermaid hair
sits on a rock; her legs will soon be long enough
to carry her away.

Sometimes the woman
lies awake
watching the fireflies bobbing
like ship's lights, the bats
with their strict radar
patrolling the dark.

The man will leave too,
one way or another,
sufficient as an old snail
carrying his small house
on his back.
She will remain, pacing

the widow's walk.
At dusk she'll pick the milky flowers
that grow by the porch stair;
she'll place them in the window,
each polished petal a star
for someone to steer home by.

25th Anniversary

There is something I want
to tell you beyond love
or gratitude or sex, beyond
irritation or a purer anger.
For years I have hoarded
your small faults the way
I might hoard kindling
towards some future conflagration,
and from the moment you broke
into my life, all out of breath,
I have half expected you
to break back out.
But here we are
like the married couple
from Cerveteri who smile
from their 6th-century sarcophagus
as if they are giving a party.
How young we were in Rome, buying
their portraits on postcards,
thinking that we too
were entangled already
beyond amputation, beyond
even death, as we are
as we are now.

Ethics

In ethics class so many years ago
our teacher asked this question every fall:
if there were a fire in a museum
which would you save, a Rembrandt painting
or an old woman who hadn't many
years left anyhow? Restless on hard chairs
caring little for pictures or old age
we'd opt one year for life, the next for art
and always half-heartedly. Sometimes
the woman borrowed my grandmother's face
leaving her usual kitchen to wander
some drafty, half-imagined museum.
One year, feeling clever, I replied
why not let the woman decide herself?
Linda, the teacher would report, eschews
the burdens of responsibility.
This fall in a real museum I stand
before a real Rembrandt, old woman,
or nearly so, myself. The colors
within this frame are darker than autumn,
darker even than winter—the browns of earth,
though earth's most radiant elements burn
through the canvas. I know now that woman
and painting and season are almost one
and all beyond saving by children.

At My Window

I have thought much
about snow,
the mute pilgrimage
of all those flakes
and about the dark wanderings
of leaves.

I have stalked
all four seasons
and seen how they beat
the same path
through the same woods
again and again.

I used to take a multitude
of trains, trusting
the strategy of tracks,
of distance.
I sailed on ships
trusting the arbitrary north.

Now I stand still
at my window
watching the snow
which knows only one direction,
falling in silence
towards silence.